CO-OPERATIVE SOCIETY MANAGEMENT AND ACCOUNTING SYSTEM

Dr Friday Ojeaburu

Copyright © 2022 Dr Friday Ojeaburu

All rights reserved

The characters and events portrayed in this book are fictitious. Any similarity to real persons, living or dead, is coincidental and not intended by the author.

No part of this book may be reproduced, or stored in a retrieval system, or transmitted in any form or by any means, electronic, mechanical, photocopying, recording, or otherwise, without express written permission of the publisher.

ISBN-13: 9798470728999

Cover design by: Art Painter
Library of Congress Control Number: 2018675309
Printed in the United States of America

CONTENTS

Title Page
Copyright
Introduction
CHAPTER 1 — 1
CHAPTER 2 — 6
CHAPTER 3 — 10
CHAPTER 4 — 13
CHAPTER 5 — 15
CHAPTER 6 — 18
CHAPTER 7 — 24
CHAPTER 8 — 27
CHAPTER 9 — 29
CHAPTER 10 — 39
CHAPTER 11 — 50
CHAPTER 12 — 53
CHAPTER 13 — 56
CHAPTER 14 — 62
CHAPTER 15 — 64
CHAPTER 16 — 67
About The Author — 73
Books By This Author — 75

INTRODUCTION

A co-operative is as old as a human being. History shows that modern co-operative society started in 1844 in Great Britain by 28 people comprising 27 males and a female, to alleviate their living conditions. They named the co-operative society Rochdale Equitable Pioneers.

The co-operative society where I was a pioneer president since 2014 is still very active and progressing from nothing to something. The cooperative disbursed over $200,000 loan facility to its member within eight years. As a result, many lives have been impacted positively.

The experience Dr. Friday Ojeaburu gained during this period is enough for this book to be a study and training material for every prospective individual who wants to start a cooperative society among their peers and friends or in the workplace with mutual interest. A co-operative remained a unique form of Business used by people & businesses for their mutual benefit,

This book is a must-read because it will answer some of the challenges faced by co-operators all around the globe.

CHAPTER 1

COOPERATIVE LAW AND PRACTICES

The earliest co-operative record originated from Fenwick, Scotland, on March 14, 1761, in a barely equipped cottage and began selling the contents at a discount, forming the Fenwick Weavers' Society.

In 1844 the Rochdale Pioneers founded the modern Co-operative Movement in Lancashire, England, to offer an affordable alternative to poor-quality and contaminated food and provisions, using any surplus to help the community. Since then, the cooperative movement has flourished, extending across the globe and encompassing all sectors of the economy.

Cooperative societies came into Nigeria in 1935 and were enacted in the same year. The 1935 ordinance, the Nigerian Co-operative Societies Ordinance of 1935, was based on the Indian model. The model was copied from the Indian Co-operative Societies Act of 1912. From here, three Co-operatives were established: Eastern Nigerian Co-operative Societies Law and Rules; Western Nigerian Co-operative Societies Law and Regulations; and Northern Nigerian Co-operative Societies Law and Regulations. We now have the Nigeria Co-operative Societies Act of 2004 after changing from Nigeria Co-operative Societies Law to Nigeria Co-operative Societies in 1993.

Today co-operative is estimated to have around 1 billion members all around the globe and employs about 250 million people worldwide directly or indirectly. Furthermore, the world's top 300 co-operatives are estimated to have a turnover of 2.2 trillion USD, as revealed by the 2014 World Co-operative Monitor.

CO-OPERATIVES

A cooperative society is a business where people who have the same common interest come together to do business to improve their living standards. International Co-operative Alliance (ICA) (2022) defined a co-operative as an autonomous association of persons united voluntarily to meet their common economic, social and cultural needs and aspirations through a jointly-owned and democratically-controlled enterprise. Cooperatives are people-centered organizations owned, controlled and run by and for their members to realize their common economic, social, and cultural requirements and aspirations. Cooperatives bring people together in a democratic and equal way. Whether the members are the customers, employees, users or residents, cooperatives are democratically managed by the 'one member, one vote' rule. Members share equal voting rights regardless of the capital they put into the enterprise.

Cooperatives permit members to take control of their economic future. Because shareholders do not own them, their activity's economic and social benefits stay in the communities where they are founded. Profits or surplus are either reinvested in the enterprise or returned to the members. The cooperative movement is far from being a marginal phenomenon; at least 12% of humanity is a cooperator of any of the 3 million cooperatives on earth (World Cooperative Monitor, 2020).

A legal instrument must be available for a cooperative society to function and are listed below:

CO-OPERATIVE LAW

The law is a vital instrument every society is expected to have and work with. This rule sets out the guidance of human conduct, which is meant for enforcement by the mechanism of the state or country. Therefore, co-operatives law states what is expected to be done and provides the legal framework as follows:

- The appointment of Director of co-operative

- The type of co-operative that must be registered
- Application requirement etc.

BYE LAW

The bye-law is a document from the individual cooperative to enable them to control themselves effectively. The bye-law is designed to suit a particular society. Information like the requirement to become a member, withdrawal or termination of a member, how to share surplus, books of account to keep etc. This state law granted the right and power to run a cooperative society in that particular state. The law must be signed by the Director of Cooperative from that state of operation.

REGULATIONS OR RULES

This regulation or rules complement the bye-law. It states the step-by-step procedures for putting the law into effect. For example, the law requires all co-operatives societies to register while the regulation or rules state the processes of such registration.

THE OBJECTIVE OF THESE INSTRUMENTS

The three legal instruments have the same aims and objectives.
1. To satisfy co-operators and stabilize development in the co-operative
2. It allows the director of co-operatives' and the co-operative societies' general house to exercise their authority
3. It makes co-operative societies have legal backing
4. It helps to protect societies from outside encroachment and against any members abusing their offices
5. It makes it possible for the cooperative fund to be used effectively and brings in accountability of funds.

CO-OPERATIVE PRINCIPLES

Voluntary and Open Membership: Co-operatives are voluntary

organizations open to all persons who can use their services and are willing to accept the responsibilities of membership without gender, social, racial, political or religious discrimination.

Democratically Control by members

Co-operatives are democratic organizations controlled by their members, who actively participate in setting their policies and making decisions. Men and women serving as elected representatives are accountable to the membership. In a co-operatives setting, every member has equal voting rights. By equal voting rights, it means one member to one vote.

Economic Participation

Members contribute equitably to fund a co-operatives society and democratically control their capital. At least part of that capital is usually the common property of the co-operatives. Members usually receive limited compensation, if any, on capital subscribed as a condition of membership. Members allocate surpluses for any or all of the following purposes measured below: development of co-operatives; building up reserves; part of which at least would be indivisible etc. Other benefits for members in the proportion of transactions with the co-operatives and any activities approved by the membership.

Autonomy and Independence

Co-operatives are autonomous, self-help organizations controlled by their members. Any time co-operatives enter into agreements with other organizations; they do so on terms that ensure democratic control by their members and maintain their co-operative's autonomy.

Education, Training and Information

Co-operatives provide education and training for their members, elected representatives, managers, and employees to contribute effectively to developing operatives. They inform the general public - particularly young people and opinion leaders - about the nature and benefits of co-operation.

Co-operation among Co-operatives
Co-operatives serve their members most effectively and strengthen the co-operatives movement by working together through local, national, regional and international structures.

Concern for Community
Co-operatives work for the sustainable development of their communities through policies approved by their members.

CHAPTER 2

TYPES OF CO-OPERATIVE SOCIETIES AND CREDIT MANAGEMENT

A Consumer Co-operative Society

It is a society established to protect the interest of general consumers. By making consumer goods available at a reasonable and affordable price. They buy goods directly from the producers or manufacturers, thereby eliminating the intermediaries in the distribution process.

A Producer Co-operative Society

It is a society established to protect the interest of small producers by making available items of their need for production like raw materials, tools and equipment, machinery, etc.

A Co-operative Marketing Society

It is a society established by small producers and manufacturers who find it difficult to sell their products individually. Therefore, society collects the products from the individual members and takes the responsibility of selling those products in the market.

A Co-operative Credit Society

It is a society established to provide financial support to its members. The organization accepts deposits from members and grants them loans at reasonable interest rates in times of need. Instances of cooperatives are Village Service Co-operative Society, Urban Cooperative Banks, Port Harcourt United Fortune Investment and Credit Society Ltd are examples of co-operatives credit societies.

A Co-operative Farming Society
It is a society formed by small farmers to work jointly and enjoy the benefits of large-scale farming.

A Housing co-operative society
Society is to buy or build a residential house for its members. The Co-operative management will purchase land, develop it, construct houses or flats, and allot the same to members. Some societies also provided loans at a low-interest rate to members to make their own homes. The Employees' Housing Societies and Metropolitan Housing Co-operatives Society are examples of housing co-operatives societies.

SOCIETIES CREDIT MANAGEMENT
Credit management in co-operative societies involves the generating fund, the disbursement of the fund to members as loans and the recovering the funds to ensure the fund are revolving. All these processes must be by the three legal instruments.

CONDITION TO OBTAIN LOAN
1. Bonafide member of the society
2. Must have a good financial record
3. Must have a minimum share required to obtain a loan
4. Must have stayed with a cooperative society with the minimum number of months stipulated by the law.
5. The members that wants a loan must submit an application in writing
6. At least two sureties shall be required before a loan can be granted
7. The purpose of the loan must be stated and approved by the committee, and the loan must use for that purpose strictly
8. The committee must determine penal interest as

stipulated in the bye-law before granting the loan.

MAXIMUM CREDIT LIMIT (MCL) AND LOAN REFUND

MCL is the higher loan any member can obtain from society. Every registered co-operative society whose objects include giving of loans can seek the approval of the general house of the co-operative society to fix the MCL. The Director of Co-operative may prescribe general or specific limits to such MCLs. Despite the MCL prescribed by the Director, the public meetings can change the MCL to suit the available members. PH United Fortune Investment and Credit Society based in Rivers State fix its MCL on times two of a member's total value of share and savings. e.g, share value of $300 and Saving Value of $200

MCL = 2 X $500=$1,000. Therefore, by MCL, each member can obtain from the society worth One Million dollars only.

INSTALMENT REFUND OF LOAN

The refund could be by monthly installment for 12 months or 24 months, or whole (at once).

ADVANTAGES
- It makes repayment east to pay
- It makes fund readily available
- It makes planning for other investment possible since more fund are available.
- It brings more surplus
- It makes the loan to circulate to more members

DISADVANTAGES
- Gradually reduces the borrower's capital investment since they have to pay from it
- Does not allow for fixed deposits
- Does not allow investment that will last for a long time.

FULL REPAYMENT

This is when loan is allowed to remain with the borrower until when is due for repayment.

ADVANTAGES
- The loan can be invested into a long business for an agreed period.
- The loan applicant can invest such loan in fixed deposit

DISADVANTAGES
- Repayment may be difficult in case of co-operative society shutdown
- Full repayment when the borrower is unable to pay may lead to poor attendance to meetings.

CHAPTER 3

FORMATION OF A CO-OPERATIVE SOCIETY

A Co-operative Society can be formed based on any country's provisions of the Co-operative Societies Act. At least ten persons can enter into a contract with common economic objectives, like farming, weaving, consuming, e.t.c. Can form a Co-operative Society. An application of interest and the society's bye-laws need to be submitted to the Registrar of Co-operative Societies of the concerned state. After scrutinizing the application and the bye-laws, the registrar issues a Certificate of Registration.

REQUIREMENTS FOR REGISTRATION

1. Choose two names of which one will be approved.
2. A minimum of 10 people is required to form co-operative
3. Application with the signature of all members
4. Bye-laws of the society are required
5. Name, address and aims and objectives of the society as stated in the bye-laws;
6. Mode of admitting new members as shown in the bye-law.
7. Share capital and its division as shown in the bye-law
8. Names, addresses and occupations of members of a minimum of 10 persons having the capacity to enter into a contract with common economic objectives
9. Passport of key EXCO like the president, treasurer and secretary.
10. Amount as specified for registration at the Ministry of Commerce and Industry.
11. Registration may be different from other states in Nigeria.

ADVANTAGES OF CO-OPERATIVE SOCIETY

Savings: It encourages saving habits in members
Easy Formation: Formation is easy compared to a joint-stock company. Any ten adults can voluntarily form an association and register it with the Registrar of co-operative societies.
Open Membership: Persons having common interests can form a cooperative society. Any competent person can become a member anytime and leave society at will.
Democratic Control: Is controlled democratically. The members cast their votes to elect their representatives to form a committee that looks after the day-to-day administration. This committee is accountable to all the members of society.
Limited Liability: The liability of members of a cooperative society is limited to the extent of their capital contributed.
Elimination of Middlemen's Profit: No need for those buying to resell. You will get items directly from suppliers and eliminate the intermediary's syndrome.
Government Assistance: From time to time, federal and state governments provide all kinds of help to societies. Such service may be provided in the form of capital contribution, loans at low-interest rates, tax exemption, subsidies in repayment of loans, etc.
Stable Life: A cooperative society has a reasonably stable life and continues to exist for a long time. It is not affected by any of its members' death, insolvency, lunacy or resignation.
Tax benefits: - To promote the Cooperative society and also the standard of living of its members, Govt. provide different tax exemptions so that tax does not become a hindrance in their growth story;

SOCIAL AND ECONOMIC IMPACTS OF CO-OPERATIVES
- Employment creation
- Credit to empower members to own their own business
- Contribution to GDP though statistics not available impact is known
- Better services to members to enable them to increase their income
- Improved business entrepreneurial skills

- Stronger cooperative identity by members, committee and managers.

CHAPTER 4

TYPES OF MEETINGS

General meeting: The law states that 'The supreme authority in a registered society shall be vested in the general meeting of members at which every member has a right to attend and vote on all questions, subject to the provision of section 25 of the act. A general meeting must not be held less than four times a year. ¼ of the members make a quorum.

First Meeting

Every society shall meet not later than one month after the receipt of its certificates of registration and shall hold a general meeting of members as its first meeting. This first meeting will help them temporarily agree on the executives and discuss some essential things that will help the co-operative.

Annual General Meeting

Every society shall hold an annual general meeting and specify the meeting as such in the notice calling for it. This meeting is held annually to discuss and approve the financial statement. Subsequently, the dividend payment can be paid to every member of the society.

Special General meeting

This may be convened at any time by the committee or director or by scrutinizer or council of inspection or at the written request of at least one-fifth of the members or delegates or twenty member's representatives, whichever is least in any of the following circumstances. Members present from the quorum.

Committee meeting

The committee shall meet as often as the business of the registered society requires and in any case, not less frequently than once a month. Half of the members makes a quorum

CHAPTER 5

CO-OPERATIVE ACCOUNTING AND LEGAL PROVISION

Co-operative accounting is the applications of financial accounting principles, concepts and policies to cooperatives in order to ascertain its financial position, promote accountability, efficient management and ensure viable operations of co-operative financial resources. The cooperative law makes the keeping of proper sets of accounting records and the preparation of the final accounts compulsory for every registered cooperative society and sets of information that must be disclosed in the final account.

The financial statement of co-operative society includes:

Income statement

the income statement reports the results of all business transactions of the cooperative that occurred during a certain time period, such as month, quarter or year. It shows the total revenue of the cooperative, the total expenses, and the resulting net income (or loss). Revenue is the amount earned by the cooperative from operations. It can come from several sources, such as selling merchandise in a supply cooperative, charging members for services or marketing their products. Cost of goods sold is the amount the cooperative paid its' supplier.

Trial balance

This is the list of account drawn up to test the arithmetical accuracy of the accounting balances. The ledgers balances are compiled into debit and credit account column totals that are equal.

Appropriation account

This is the part that deal with how the surplus is shared among dividend, interest, bonus, reserve, honoraria, education fund and general reserve.

Statement of financial position

The statement of financial position also known as balance sheet is used to report the financial position of the cooperative at a given point in time, usually at the end of a month, quarter, or year. It shows the assets owned by the cooperative balanced against its liabilities and member equity. Assets are listed on the right-hand side of a balance sheet while liabilities and member equity are listed on the left-hand side.

Cash flow statements

As its name indicates, only those accounts that result in cash flowing in or out of the cooperative during the accounting period are included on the statement of cash flows. This report shows the change that occurred in amount of cash from the opening to the closing of the cooperative's balance sheets. We have three categories on the statement of cash flows: operations, investment transactions, and financing transactions. Cash flow from operations gives the net cash from providing goods and services to members and all other cash flows not from investment or financing transactions. This includes net income, adjustments to net income, and changes in balance sheet items. Adjustments to net income offset the non-cash items included on the income statement that do not result in an actual inflow or outflow of cash, such as depreciation, a gain (loss) from the sale of an asset, and deferred taxes. Changes in balance sheet items are assets and liabilities where changes result in positive or negative cash flows, such as accounts receivable, accounts payable, patronage refunds payable, or other accrued expenses. Cash flow from investment transactions include the purchase or sale of property and equipment, the purchase or redemption of equity in other organizations, and payments from long-term investments. Cash flow from financing transactions include the acquisition or redemption of loans, the sale of capital stock, redemption of member equities or payment of patronage refunds.

BOOKKEEPING

Cooperative society is a legal entity. It may own properties like furniture, landed properties, buildings, motor vehicle, equipment etc. in the course of their financial transactions, they incur expenses. These financial transactions involve exchange of money. The recording of these financial transaction is called bookkeeping. Example of bookkeeping transaction are recording banking transaction, recording of loan to members, recording of expenses etc.

LEGAL PROVISION

The cooperative law of Nigeria makes the keeping of proper books of accounting records compulsory. The same law also made the preparation of the financial statement compulsory for every registered cooperative society. It also made it mandatory for the accounts of the society to be audited by and auditor and a copy send to the Director of cooperative society in the state of operation.

The account should specifically cover the income and expenditure account, statement of financial position, statement of cash flow, receipt and payment etc. failures to keep these set of account could attract penalty of six-month imprisonment.

CHAPTER 6

ACCOUNTING CONCEPTS

Accounting concepts are broad basic assumptions that underline the preparation of periodic financial accounts of business enterprises. The basics concepts are

GOING CONCERN CONCEPT

accounting assumes that the business will continue to operate for an extended period. This while society will give members loans for up to two years and do business that will take long years to complete. In other words, it means continuity in business or Continuity Assumption. For example, prepayment and accrual expenses occur in society because of the belief that society will continue operations in the future. Therefore, going concerned applies to the whole society, unlike when such a cooperative society closes one of its branches or discontinues one revenue line.

BUSINESS ENTITY CONCEPT

This means the business is a legal entity. It can sue and be sued. It also means the business owners are limited to how much he has invested, not their resources. In the case of society, the shareholders can only lose the value of shares contributed to the business. So, for example, if the shareholder or member brings in $10,000 share contributions into the industry, we will treat this as part of the total shares and sum it up as a liability on the statement of financial position of the business.

DUAL CONCEPTS

this says that there are two aspects of accounting. That is, givers and receivers. These two aspects are always equal to each other.

It is represented by the business's assets and liabilities (i.e., claims against it). Assets = liabilities + capital. So, for example. Say the society buys an asset worth $10 000. So now, the non-current assets of the society will increase by $10 000. But at the same time, the bank or cash balance will reduce by $10 000, so the transaction will have a dual effect in accounting. And also, the statement of financial position will stay balanced.

REALIZATION CONCEPTS

in accounting, profit should not be recognized until the goods are passed to the customer. For example, in advance payment of services. A customer pays $12,000 in advance for a full year of Generator Maintenance. Society does not realize the $12,000 of revenue until it has performed work. This can be defined as the passage of time, so the society could initially record the entire $12,000 as a liability and post it to the unearned revenue account and then shift $1,000 of it per month to revenue by debiting the unearned revenue account

MONEY MEASUREMENT CONCEPT

Accounting is only concerned with the facts that can be measured in monetary terms with a fair degree of objectivity. Accounting does not record that the society has a bad or good management team, poor morale among staff but in only naira and kobo. For example, a society that owns $100,000 cash, 130 tons of raw material, 20 vehicles and 100 acres of land cannot be added or subtracted together and will never make a meaningful conclusion. However, a decision can be reached if we express the above items in monetary terms. Another example is that loyal, hardworking and punctual workers that play a significant role in the profitability and growth of the society cannot be written as an asset of the society and cannot be expressed in money terms.

ACCRUAL CONCEPT

Revenue and cost are usually recorded in accounts when they are earned or incurred rather than when the money is received or paid. The Accruals concept ensures that all revenues and expenses are recognized within the correct reporting period, irrespective of the timing of the related cash flow. It is sometimes referring to the matching concept, for example, in the case of sales accrual. For example, a services society has several employees working on a significant project for the federal government, which it will bill when the project has been completed. In the meantime, the society can accrue revenue for the work completed to date, even though it has not yet been billed.

Another example is a utility company that records the expenses of $2,000 for providing the monthly service. It records the revenue of $2,000 when it posts the customer bill at the end of the month, even though the customer hasn't submitted a payment. Therefore, for that month of service, the accountant records the expenses and accrues revenue on the statement of financial position even if the customer has not yet submitted payment.

FULL DISCLOSURE CONCEPT

This concept states that all relevant information will be disclosed in the accounting statements. Many external users depend on these financial statements for their data to make investing decisions. So no information/transactions relevant to any of them will be omitted from these statements for the company's benefit. For example, if society expects a change in the tax rate in the nearest future or wants to change IFRS reporting, it must disclose this information appropriately. Also, every society must disclose the accounting policies and methods used for preparing its financial statements to the users of financial statements.

COST CONCEPT

This accounting concept states that all firm assets are entered into the books of account at their purchase price, such as cost of acquisition + transport + installation). The price remains the same (minus depreciation charged). The cost concept states that items must be recorded as the actual price. It believes in having a record equal to the amount paid for the item. It is the same as when a buyer buys products, and the recording is done based on the price. In short, the cost principle equals the amount paid for each transaction. For example, if you spend $20,000 to buy a car for a cooperative society office, the record should record $20,000. Even if the vehicle is later valued at $30,000, the form will still show $20,000 or even something lower because of depreciation. This is because the asset's market price is not considered.

ACCOUNTING PERIOD CONCEPT

Every organization, according to its needs, chooses a specific period to complete an accounting cycle. Generally, the time chosen is a year we call the accounting year. The period is mentioned in the financial statements. For example, a cooperative society can choose an annual fiscal year such as July 1, 2020, through June 30, 2021; April 1, 2020, through March 31, 2021.

ACCOUNTING CONVENTION

This common practice is used as a guideline when recording a business transaction. In addition, it is used when there is no definitive guideline in the accounting standards governing a specific situation. Thus, accounting conventions fill in the gaps not yet addressed by accounting standards.

CONSISTENCY

It refers to using the same methods for the same items (i.e., consistency of treatment) either from period to period within a reporting entity or in a single period across entities. Or the principle of accounting says that the same accounting policies and procedures should be followed in every accounting period. Constantly changing the methods of reporting profit would lead to a distortion of the profits calculated from the accounting records.

CONSERVATISM

The accountant will take a figure that will understate rather than overstate the profit. Record losses in the books but don't anticipate profit prematurely. An alternative term, which means the same, is prudence. Prudence Concept: not expecting profits until it has been realized. For example, if society buys landed property worth 45m per land, this should be recorded in the statement of financial position at cost. Now, assuming that the land's market price is $7m per land. In reality, a gain of $2m per land has been made, but it is unrealized because the land has not been sold by the financial position date. The prudence principle requires that this be ignored because it has not been realized. But continually showing the land as $5m per land in the book with a note to the account to say that their market value is higher than their cost. However, should the importance of this land go below $5m per share to $4m per land on the financial position date, it would be prudent to book the loss in the record. For the loss case, let's assume that on the financial position date, the land is being sold at the stock exchange at $4m per land. It is prudent to book a loss of $1m per land and show the land at $1m in the statement of financial position even though the loss has not been incurred (i.e., because the land is still held by the business and their value is likely to change in the future).

MATERIALITY

Information is material if. Omitting it or misstating it could influence decisions that users make based on financial information about a specific reporting entity. For instance, a $5,000 amount will likely be immaterial for a sizeable cooperative society with a net income of $90,000. However, the same $5,000 amount will be material for a small society with a net income of $9,000. Materiality and a matching concept clash at this point. For example, the materiality concept believes the company can expend $50 wastebasket for a year instead of depreciating it over its useful life of 5 years. But the matching principles direct the recording of wastebasket as an asset and then reporting depreciation expenses of $10 a year for five years. Instead, materiality allows you to expense the entire $50 cost in the year it is acquired. The reason is that no investor, creditor, or another interested party would be misled by immediately expensing the $50 wastebasket.

CHAPTER 7

IMPORTANCE OF CO-OPERATIVE ACCOUNTING

To staff

   a. Once trained, the staff obtain necessary knowledge and skills that empower them to record and maintain the books of accounts effectively
   b. Once trained, the staff can be located in any department of the society to release bookkeeping and other accounting functions
   c. When structures are correctly put in place, staff don't have to spend a lot of time asking colleagues what to do
   d. Because of the setting, specific training to man and operate the co-op accounting system can be offered to the staff at a central point.
   e. Staff can readily account for their day-to-day activities and vindicate their continued employment.
   f. The staff can work more efficiently in their area of specialization.

To co-operative society

Proper accounting is put in place; society's assets and liabilities are safeguarded adequately.

   a. Exact financial position of society is known
   b. It enables society to discover how much money it owes outsiders and how much outsiders owe the society.
   c. Enable society to calculate its surplus or losses at any given period.
   d. Effective decision-making is maintained
   e. There is a cost-saving in auditing fees.
   f. It ensures accurate records of financial transactions are

well-captured
g. With accurate records, negotiation of loan is made easy
h. It enables for comparison with previous years.
i. The management can justify continued members' investment in the co-op society.
j. It is easier to calculate members' claims with accurate records.
k. Proper records of past events help with plans.
l. It helps to determine the efficiency of management and stability of the society.
m. The co-op can meet the legal requirements, especially those under the co-op society Act

To members

a. It assists the members to produce more by providing the necessary input and training to them
b. Members are well informed of their co-op transactions on a timely basis
c. Members can justify, i.e., rationalize, the undertaking of certain co-op investments which affect their economic welfare.
d. Each member can get a fair share of bonus or dividends in the proportion of shares invested and volume of business transacted
e. Members are happy to see that their affairs are run fairly and transparently and therefore minimize organizational politics

To trainee

a. Co-op accounting is highly specialized in that one can only learn it in a co-op training course and apply it precisely in a a co-op society
b. There are managers, and qualified accountants who have no orientation on the subject and do not fully understand what the issue entails and they are faced with some problems in the process of preparing the

books of accounts
c. The training thereby enables one to be helpful within the co-op movement as one can fulfill roles and obligations within the co-operative society
d. Co-operative accounting is essential to the trainee because:
- Working as a co-op accounting trainer or co-op accounting system consultant
- Acting as a financial adviser to any co-op society
- Being an asset and liability management consultant in a co-op organization
- By taking a further course in accounting, especially in co-op accounting and auditing

CHAPTER 8

SOURCES OF COOPERATIVE FUND

Entrance/Re-entrance fees

The amount paid to be a member of the society. This money should be settled once in a lifetime except for those who re-join the society after resigning or withdrawing from membership. This category of person has to pay to renew their membership. This money is non-refundable.

Share capital

This is the stake, interest, or personal belonging a member has in the cooperative. It is a member's part of liability in society. This is what members can lose in case of liquidation of the cooperative. This form member's total contribution when added to the share contribution. In case members need a loan, members' savings and share contributions will be added to the total contribution.

Member's savings

This personal belonging to a member attracts interest to the member payout of the surplus declared at the end of the year. This also forms members' total contribution when added to the shared gift. If members need a loan, members' savings and share contributions will be added to the total contribution.

Reserves

This is the amount set aside from the cooperative's surplus to strengthen the business's financial position. What is set aside for reserves must be stated in the bye-law as one way to distribute surplus. This section of the bye-law can be amended to reflect what the general house wants.

Borrowed capital
This is the money borrowed from members, outsiders or banks to execute a specific project. This fund needs to be serviced by paying interest which comes as a cost to society.

Deposits and loans from members
These are deposits from members which attract interest payable by the cooperative. This part of the deposit does not attract dividends but only interest, which must be paid before determining the compensation for the year. This can be withdrawn on short notice.

Other sources
This is like fine or levy for late coming, fine or levy for unruly behavior, fine or levy for fighting in a meeting.

REQUIREMENTS TO OPEN A BANK ACCOUNT
1. Society resolution to open such an account.
2. Photocopy of Bye-Law of the Society while original sighted
3. 1 passport photograph for each signatory
4. Means of ID for all signatories
5. Any payment showing the address of the society
6. Signature mandate card
7. Opening balance (depending on the bank).

CHAPTER 9

BOOK AND RECORDS IN COOPERATIVE

Like any other businesses, cooperative societies are required to keep proper records and books of accounts of their business transaction. The success and failures of a cooperative society depend on properly maintaining records and books of accounts.

PURPOSE OF ACCOUNTING BOOKS AND RECORDS

They are listed below
1. It helps refresh the memory about past business activities of the society and also serves for future references.
2. It reveals the actual financial position of a cooperative society.
3. It helps the management committee members decide on future policies and programmes.
4. It helps in the prevention and detection of frauds and errors.
5. It makes the society to be creditworthiness
6. It gives more confidence to the existing members.
7. It attracts new members to join through referrals and society's past achievements.
8. It helps the society to confirm claims by members, customers and creditors regarding finance.

TYPES OF ACCOUNT BOOKS AND RECORD

Accounts and records shall be maintained in the forms prescribed by the registrar, and more to be added by the society shall include the following as seen below:

1. **MEMBER'S PASSBOOK**

A passbook is opened for every member who serves as a personal account on which all transactions between a member and the society are recorded. This forms part of the subsidiary ledger account. This is for individual members, who always produce it for recording their contribution of shares, savings, and contribution balances as a most common transaction on the passbook. Study the template below for more clarification

Cover page

ABC INVESTMENT & CREDIT SOCIETY LTD
NO 21EMEKUKU STREET, D/LINE, PORT HARCOURT, RIVERS STATE

MEMBER'S PASSBOOK

NAME..
NO..
ADDRESS..
DATE ISSUED...

Back page

NOTE
A passbook will be bought by a new member or when exhausted. It remains the property of the society and must be surrendered on exhaustion of when membership ceases.
While in the hands of the member, it must be carefully preserve and produced when required. A lost passbook must be replaced by new one showing the latest balance on payment of the cost. The letter "D" should be entered in the "particulars" column to indicate a deposit similarly if savings are withdrawn the letter "W" should be entered in its column. Loans and fixed deposits be entirely distinct transactions are not entered in the members passbook and do not affect his balance as shown therein.

Inside page

Date	Particulars	Debit $	Credit $	Balance $	Treasurer's Signature

1. ANALYSIS BOOK

This is used to record members' contributions, disbursed loans and repayment, membership withdrawal, fines and other monthly incomes. This book helps to analyze the transaction every month. Moreover, this book helps cooperative to always spread open in front of members at any general meeting of the society.

S/N	Names	Entrance fee($)	Shares($)	Savings($)	Fine($)	Loan Disbursement($)	Loan Rec($)	Interest on Loan($)	Withdrawal($)	Withdrawal fee($)
1	ABC	50	100	30	5	500				
2	XYZ	50	200	20			40	5		
3	BB	50	40	10			50	6		
4	VV	50	50	10	10				45	5
5	MM	50	60	10						
6	JJ	50	70	10		600				
7	LL	50	80	20						
Total		350	600	110	15	1100	90	11	45	5

2. CASH RECEIPT

This helps to record all money received in cash or in a cheque. This official receipt supports financial transactions as evidence that money has been received on behalf of society. All receipts must be serially numbered and used in that order. The receipt bears the following date of receipt; amount both in figure and words; receipt number; the society's name and official rubber stamp; the name of the payee; receiving office signature. The receipt is prepared in triplicate and distributed as original, duplicate and triplicate copies. The original goes with the payee. Duplicate to the accounts section, and triplicate remains a book copy and should not be perforated. It is used for auditing purposes. Receipts are used complete the Cash Account. It is evidence that money has been received in favor of the society

ABC Cooperative	
20, Aba Road, PH	
Cash Receipt No................. Date....................	
Received from..	
Sum of..Naira..........Kobo...	
In Respect of:	
Shares	
Entrance fee	
Ordinary Savings	
Special Savings	
Member's Loan	
Advances	
Treasurer Sign..................................	
Total Amount	

3. EQUIPMENT RECORD

These records are used to record all the cooperative society's capital assets, such as landed properties, vehicles, office furniture, building etc.

4. CASHBOOK

This is a book where receipts and payments of money are recorded. It helped record all transactions either in cash or in the society's cheques, including receipts and expenditures with balances at the end of the period. The source documents for this book are the receipt book, the payment voucher and the general ledger. The essence of the cask book is to ascertain the cash balance with the treasurer and the bank at every given period.

Date	Particular	Folio	Cash($)	Bank($)	Date	Particular	Folio	Cash($)	Bank($)
Jan	Bal B/d		20	300					
	Share			600		Loan Disbursement			1100
	Savings			110		Withdrawal			45
	Entrance		100	250					
	Fine			15					
	Loan Rec			90		Telephone		10	
	Interest Received			11					
	Withdrawal fee			5		Bal C/D		110	236
			120	1381				120	1381

5. GENERAL LEDGER

This book contains individual accounts for transactions of a business organization. e.g., Share account, Bank Charges, Telephone, Rent Account. This account is created on a periodical basis and is the final destination of all the entries reported in the subsidiary book of account. The general ledger is to show at any given time the total income generated or expenses incurred on a particular transaction item. It has columns, as shown below.

Telephone

S/N	Date	Particular	Folio	Amount($)	Balance($)
1	1/2/2017	Recharge		6	
2	20/2/2017	Recharge		4	10

6. CERTIFICATE OF REGISTRATION

This is the law of the state that backs a cooperative society. It gave the society to be a corporate body, which can now sue and be sued. It gives cooperative evidence that it has the right to operate within the state. If a cooperative wants to work in the whole state, then such a cooperative must need to register with Corporate Affairs Commission (CAC).

7. PERSONAL LEDGER

This ledger helps to record members' contributions of shares, savings, deposits, withdrawals, loans and refunds. The entries into this book are from the individual's transaction that is seen in the analysis book, which is also entered in the passbook. With the proper recording of transactions, individual cash balances can be seen at a glance. This book shows the individual cash balance at a glance

ABC Co-operative Society

Serial No: Date of Admission: Members:
Name: Date of Cessation: Signature:
           Reason:

Date	Particular	Ref	Share			Savings			Total	Fine	Loan			Loan Interest	Deposit			Authentication
			Dr.($)	Cr.($)	Balance ($)	Dr.($)	Cr.($)	Balance ($)			Dr.($)	Cr.($)	Balance ($)		Dr.($)	C4($)	Balance($)	

8. BYE LAW

This state law granted the right and power to run a cooperative society in that particular state. The law must be signed by the Director of Cooperative from that state of operation.

9.   THE CO-OPERATIVE ACT

This Act or Law gave birth to cooperative bye-law and made the registration and operation of cooperative societies throughout the Federation of a nation possible and prosperous.

10.   LOAN BOND

This could be a template already written loan agreement that members complete when funds are advanced to them as loans. Where there is no such template, loan applicants are expected to apply with a handwritten application for a loan. The essence is to show the bond between the member and the society when a loan is granted. Moreover, it helps to regulate who should be held responsible in the case of defaults. Loan Committee can manage this.

LOAN BOND
ABC Cooperative
I, ...hereby acknowledge receipt from named society................................... ....Being a loan bearing interest at .... per annum for the purpose of ....
I promise to use the loan only for the purpose stated above and understand that i must refund the loan in full on demand. If i use it for any other purposes, otherwise i agree to refund the money with interest.   a. .(the principal to be written)   b. In ....equal instalment   c. Each is commencing 0n ....at intervals of 12 months   d. Therefore until..
Security for the loan, 1 hereby pledge   a. The under mentioned crop/street/livestock   b. The under mentioned property
Section 53(2) of the cooperative society's law has been brought to my notice   Witness to Signature   Signature & Date of Borrower

Back page
We...and ....
Undertake to ensure that the loan is used by borrower for purpose named in this bond and further undertake to repay the loan together with any interest excluding penal interest, that may due to the society should the borrower fail or be unable to do so either in cash or in accordance with the bond.
Section 53(2) of the cooperative society's law has been brought to our notice
First Surety.................................... Date ....
Second Surety.................................... Date...............................
Cancellation of Bond
Loan repaid and Bond Cancelled
Date..   Secretary Comment..

9. LOAN REGISTER

It is a source document containing information regarding all loans granted at any time by the management committee or credit or loan committee meeting. Such information includes personal membership number; member identity number, committee meeting minute number, cheque number; amount authorized and approved; amount applied for; Amount granted; date of approval, period of the loan and date of refund. This schedule will also be used to post the cash book and member personal account. The total figure on the cheque schedule will also be used for direct casting to the society's check register. Authority to pay out when the credit or loan committee approves a loan is by the chairman and member of the credit or loan committee signing on the application form. Cheque signatories on the cheque schedule endorse further approval of check payment. All the cheques must be individually listed on the cash receipt, cash disbursement journal and cash journal. The cheque loan schedule should be prepared in the triplicate and distributed as follows. -Original goes to the account section. -Duplicate goes to the bank -Triplicate is left as a copy.

Membership personal number:

Member identity number:

Committee meeting minute number:

LOAN REGISTER						
Name of Borrower	Amount Applied for	Amount Granted	Date of approval	Period of Loan	Date of refund	Remarks
Juan M	$1,000	$1,000	12/1/2018	12	30/12/2018	Cleared
Fred G	$1,500	$1,000	20/1/2019	12	On-going	On-going

10. CHEQUE BOOKS AND SAVING BOOKLET

Cooperative is expected to open an account in their name immediately after approval is granted by the Director of the Cooperative in the respective state of Nigeria. Every cash payment and receipt is made through the banking system.

11. PAYMENT VOUCHERS

It is prepared to support payment in many organizations. A cheque payment voucher is ready to help and evidence all monies paid out by the management of the cooperative society. Before any cheque is written, the authority must be sought from the president or chief executive, as the case may be for payment and loans. In addition, the officer authorized the payment vouchers. Each time a cheque is paid, the document is prepared in triplicate. -Original to the account section -Duplicate the payee -Triplicate remains as a book copy - The payment voucher would show the Name of the society; Cheque number and amount; Payee name; Identification and physical address. For recording, all monies are paid out from the cooperative to meet expenses.

ABC Cooperative	
20, Aba Road, PH	
Payment Voucher Date..................	
Pay to...	
Sum of...Naira..........Kobo...	
Description	
Total amount	
Prepared by................................	Approved by.............
Date	Date

11. CORRESPONDENCE FILE

This is another crucial record in cooperative which makes communication easy with cooperative societies and other business partners.

12. BANK PAY-IN SLIP

It is a statement that instructs the bank to credit society accounts with deposits made. It also serves as a source document for society records. Therefore, it should be well kept for future reference.

13. ANNUAL FINANCIAL REPORT

This is the report to be submitted to the general house at the Annual General Meetings. It must be extracted from the books of account and presented to the general house. The annual financial report consists of a statement of financial position, a statement of cash flow and a statement of income and expenditure (or statement of profit or loss and other comprehensive income).

14. SHARES REGISTER

All members' shares, contributions and withdrawals are captured in the share register. The share register is vital since it shows evidence of the named shareholder's legal title to the shares in the co-operative, subject to any evidence to the contrary. Cooperative treats the person named in the share register as the registered holder of the relevant shares. Such a person is only entitled to exercise the voting rights that attach to the shares, to receive notices, to receive distributions of dividends in respect of the ratio of the shares holding, and to exercise any other rights and powers that attach to the shares.

CHAPTER 10

FORMAT OF ANNUAL FINANCIAL STATEMENT

Following this format demonstrated in this chapter, you will be able to prepare your co-operative account without engaging an expert's services.

COVER PAGE

ABC CO-OPERATIVE INVESTMENT & CREDIT SOCIETY LTD
FINANCIAL STATEMENT 2018

CONTENT

Financial report for the year ended, 30 November 2018

Contents	Pages
Corporate information	1
Report of the management committee	2
Statement of accounting policies	3
Statement of income and expenditure account	4
Statement of financial position	5
Statement of cash flow	6
Financial result at a glance	7
Notes to the accounts	8-10

CORPORATE INFORMATION
MANAGEMENT COMMITTEE

Dr Friday Ojeaburu.	President	(fix date elected)
Mr Fred Goddy.	General Secretary	(fix date elected)
Mrs Juan Moses	Financial Secretary	(fix date elected)
Dr Esther Kings	Treasurer	(fix date elected)
Mrs Ruth James	Ass. Secretary	(fix date elected)

REGISTERED OFFICE: C/o President,
10 Aba Road,
PH, Rivers State.

COOPERATIVE SOCIETY REGISTRATION NO: RvNo 110563.

BANKERS   First Bank Plc

FINANCIAL REPORT OF THE MANAGEMENT COMMITTEE FOR THE YEAR ENDED 30 NOVEMBER, 2018

The Management Committee has the pleasure in submitting, to the members of the Society their Financial Report for the year ended 30 November, 2018.

LEGAL FORM

The Society commenced operations on 12th January 2000 and was incorporated as a Cooperative Society. It was registered at Rivers State Cooperative Society under Section 10 of the Cooperative Society Law (Chapter 29) of Rivers State of Nigeria.

PRINCIPAL ACTIVITIES

The principal activity of the Society is investment, Thrift and Credit operations. Also carries out giving of loan to members.

MANAGEMENT COMMITTEE'S RESPONSIBILITY

In accordance with provisions of the Nigerian Cooperative Societies Act 98 of 1993 (now an Act of 2004), the Management Committee is responsible for the preparation of annual financial statements which gives a true and fair view of the state of affairs of the Society at the end of each financial period and of the profit or loss for that period to ensure that:

- Proper accounting books and records are maintained by the Society.
- Applicable accounting standards are followed.
- Suitable accounting policies supported by reasonable and prudent judgements' and estimates are consistently followed in preparing the financial statements.
- The going concern basis is used, unless it is inappropriate to presume that the Society will continue in business.
- Internal control procedures are instituted which will reasonably safeguard the Society's assets, prevent and detect fraud and other irregularities.

BY ORDER OF THE COMMITTEE

Dr Friday Ojeaburu	Mr Fred Goddy
President........................	General Secretary.............................

Mrs Juan Moses
Financial Secretary……………..

Dr Esther Kings
Treasurer……………………….
………..

Mrs Ruth James

Ass. Secretary…………………..
……..

STATEMENT OF ACCOUNTING POLICIES

The following summarizes the significant accounting policies applied by the Society in arriving at the accompanying accounts.

1. BASIS OF ACCOUNTING

The accounts are prepared under the historical cost convention modified by the revaluation of certain investment assets and complies with the Statements of Accounting Standard issued by the Financial Reporting Council (formerly Nigerian Accounting Standards Board).

2. INCOME RECOGNITION

(i) Interest Income on loan is realised on a monthly basis from the month of loan disbursement.
(ii) Sales of items are made at profit.

3. PROPERTY, PLANT AND EQUIPMENT (PPE)

All categories of property, plant and equipment are initially recorded at cost. Subsequent costs are included in the asset carrying amount or recognized as a separate asset as appropriate only when it is probable that future economic benefits associated with the item will flow to the Cooperative, and the cost of the item can be measured reliably. Property, Plant and equipment (PPE) are stated at cost less accumulated depreciation. Depreciation is provided on a straight-line basis at rates calculated to write off the cost of each asset over its estimated useful life at the following annual rate

Asset Category Rates	%
Office equipment	25
Other Assets	20

4. DIVIDEND TO MEMBERS

Dividend to members is calculated on members' total shares balances and is deemed paid when credited to members' bank accounts annually after approval at Annual General Meeting (AGM).

5. INTEREST ON SAVINGS TO MEMBERS

Interest on Savings to members is calculated on members' total savings balances and is deemed paid when credited to members' bank accounts annually after approval at Annual General Meeting (AGM).

STATEMENT OF INCOME AND EXPENDITURE ACCOUNT FOR THE YEAR ENDED 30th NOVEMBER, 2018

CO-OPERATIVE SOCIETY MANAGEMENT AND ACCOUNTING SYSTEM

	Notes	2018 $
Revenue		
Interest on Loan		4,500,000.00
Interest on Salary Advance		80,000.00
Land Commission		3,400,000.00
Equipment Item Income	1	85,096.93
Other Revenue	2	436,448.40
Welfare Levy	15	191,000.00
Total Revenue		**7,692,545.33**
Less Expenses:		
Bank Charges		250,000.00
Interest Payable		10,000.00
Administrative Expenses	3	1,131,677.75
Welfare Expenses	15	133,250.00
Total Expenses		**1,524,927.75**
Surplus (Deficit) for the year		6,167,617.58
Appropriation of surplus fund:		
Dividend		690,000.00
Interest paid to members		460,000.00
Reserve fund		230,000.00
Bonus		644,000.00
Education Fund		46,000.00
Honorarium		230,000.00
General Reserve		3,809,867.58
Welfare Fund		57,750.00
		6,167,617.58

STATEMENT OF FINANCIAL POSITION AS AT 30th NOVEMBER, 2018

DR FRIDAY OJEABURU

	Notes	2018 $	2018 $
Non-Current Asset			
Property, Plant and Equipment	4		**1,584,000**
Current Asset			
Cash and cash equivalent			(1,741,416.65)
Account Receivables	6		922,272.31
Loan Account	7		23,611,532.00
Salary Advance	8		3,657,266.97
Commodity Advance	9		(1,397,928.25)
Electronic Item Advance			916,647.77
			25,968,374.15
Current Liability			
Honorarium		230,000.00	
Interest Payable		10,000.00	
Bonus		644,000.00	
Dividend		690,000.00	
Interest paid to members		460,000.00	
Account Payables	5	470,017.50	(2,504,017.50)
Net Current Asset			23,464,356.65
Net Asset			**25,048,356.65**
Accumulated funds:			
Members Fund	10		22,334,716.97
Reserve fund	11		(689,750.00)
General Reserve	12		4,549,466.58
Education Fund	13		(83,000.00)
Land Contribution Fund	14		(1,182,326.90)
Welfare Fund	15		119,250.00
Net Asset			**25,048,356.65**

STATEMENT OF CASH FLOW FOR THE YEAR ENDED 30th NOVEMBER, 2018

CO-OPERATIVE SOCIETY MANAGEMENT AND ACCOUNTING SYSTEM

		2018
		$
Surplus After Depreciation		6,167,617.58
Add back: Depreciation		207,700.00
		6,375,317.58
Changes in Working Capital		
Interest Payable		10,000.00
Account Receivables		353,673.69
Account Payables		470,017.50
Loan Account	8	(3,028,740.00)
Salary Advance	9	(2,487,316.97)
Commodity Advance		3,328,543.50
Electronic Item Advance	15	(916,647.77)
Welfare Fund	16	57,750.00
		4,162,597.53
Cash Flow from Investing Activities		
Purchase of non- current asset		(2,725,750.00)
Members Fund		9,506,253.22
Land Contribution Fund		(1,851,226.90)
Special Savings		(600,000.00)
Dividend		(1,290,000.00)
Interest paid to members		(731,000.00)
Bonus		(1,290,000.00)
Honorarium		(430,000.00)
Welfare Fund		(57,750.00)
Net cash flow		4,693,123.85
Cash & cash equivalent, beginning of year		(6,434,540.50)
Cash & cash equivalent, end of year		**(1,741,416.65)**

FINANCIAL RESULT AT A GLANCE

DR FRIDAY OJEABURU

	2018 $	2017 $	2016 $	2015 $
Revenue				
Interest on Loan	4,500,000.00	3,166,000.00	1,698,570.00	193,520.00
Interest on Salary Advance	80,000.00	105,460.00	26,900.00	------------
Land Commission	3,400,000.00	1,340,000.00	1,596,000.00	------------
Equipment Item Income	85,096.93	429,024.00	99,726.25	------------
Other Revenue	436,448.40	785,349.00	23,216.00	------------
Welfare Levy	191,000.00	111,900	429,746.17	98,000.00
	7,692,545.33	**5,937,733.00**	**3,874,158.42**	**291,520.00**
Expenses:				
Bank Charges	250,000.00	195,090.95	56,625.69	10,334.00
Interest Payable	10,000.00	131,130.00	------------	------------
Administrative Expenses	1,131,677.75	1,166,750.00	634,800.00	90,040.00
Welfare Expenses	133,250.00	50,000.00		
Total Expenses	**1,524,927.75**	**1,542,970.95**	**691,405.69**	**100,374.00**
Surplus for the year	6,167,617.58	4,393,262.05	3,182,752.73	191,146.00
Appropriation of surplus fund:				
Proposed Dividend	690,000.00	1,290,000.00	632,435.01	80,000.00
Proposed Interest	460,000.00	731,000.00	411,082.76	60,000.00
Reserve fund	230,000.00	430,000.00	758,922.01	10,000.00
Proposed Bonus	644,000.00	1,290,000.00	949,846.52	10,000.00
Education Fund	46,000.00	129,000.00	94,865.25	------------
Honoraria	230,000.00	430,000.00	316,217.51	20,000.00
General Reserve	3,809,867.58	33,262.05	19,383.67	11,146.00
Welfare Fund	57,750.00	61,500.00		
	6,167,617.58	**4,393,262.05**	**3,182,752.73**	**191,146.00**
Members Fund	22,334,716.97	21,341,193.75	8,512,730.00	2,846,000.00

NOTES TO THE FINANCIAL STATEMENTS FOR YEAR ENDED 30 NOVEMBER, 2018

CO-OPERATIVE SOCIETY MANAGEMENT AND ACCOUNTING SYSTEM

		2017 $	2018 $
1	**Equipment Items**		
	Paid to Suppliers	---------	2,013,827.75
	Receipt from Members	---------	2,098,924.68
	Surplus(Deficit)	---------	85,096.93
2	**Other Revenue**		
	Fine & Default fee	282,410	262,381.55
	Other fine Charges	381,729	70,000
	Entrance fees	64,000	22,000
	Administrative Fee	49,210	37,700
	Membership withdrawal fee	8,000	44,366.85
		785,349.00	**436,448.40**
3	**Administrative Expenses**		
	Entertainment Cost	180,000	41,200
	Transport & Travelling Cost	142,240	49,000
	Sundry Expenses	41,972	185,700
	Office Expenses	248,710	259,700
	AGM Expenses	185,700	268,000
	Sitting Allowance	216,128	103,877.75
			47,877.75
	Depreciation	101,700	207,700
		1,166,750.00	**1,131,677.75**
4	**Property, Plant and Equipment**		
	Cost		
	At 1 January	122,400	731,700
	Additions in the year	711,000.	1,060,000
	At 30 November,	**833,400**	**1,791,700**
	Depreciation		
	At 1 January	30,600	101,700
	Charges for the year	71,100	106,000.00
	At 30 November,	**101,700**	**207,700.00**
	Net Book Value		
	At 30 November	**731,700**	**1,584,000**
5	**Account Payable**		
	Outsider		470,017.50

6	**Accounts Receivables**		
	Interest on Salary Advance	9,500	26,400
	Interest on Loan	368,500	519,000
	Commodity Items	252,157	
	Land commission	264,000	130,000
	Other Incomes	381,729	213,046
	Equipment	-----------	33,826.31
		1,275,946.00	**922,272.31**
7	**Loan Account**		
	Balance, beginning of the year	6,851,629	20,582,792
	Loan to Members	33,401,000	32,672,000
	Loan Recovered	(19,669,837)	(29,643,260)
	Balance, end of the year	**20,582,792.00**	**23,611,532.00**
8	**Salary Advance**		
	Balance, beginning of the year	--------------	1,169,950.00
	Advance to Members	4,148,000	4,584,066.97
	Advance Recovered	(2,978,000)	(2,096,750.00)
	Balance, end of the year	**1,169,950.00**	**3,657,266.97**
9	**Commodity Advance**		
	Balance b/d	-----------	1,930,615.25
	Advance to purchase commodity	4,709,245.00	-------------
	Advance recovered from members	2,778,629.75	3,328,543.50
	Balance c/d	**1,930,615.25**	**(1,397,928.25)**

10 **Members fund** This represents the indebtedness of the Cooperative to its members in the form of the credit balance in member's fund account as at the end of the year under review.

10a	**Ordinary Shares**		
	Balance, beginning of year		6,540,680.00
	Shares contributed during the year	6,714,500	6,277,985.22
	Withdrawal during the year	(173,900)	(2,183,451.25)
	Balance, end of the year	**6,540,680.00**	**10,635,213.97**
10b	**Ordinary Savings**		
	Balance, beginning of year		6,287,783.75
	Savings during the year	8,502,183.75	11,409,380
	Withdrawal during the year	(2,214,400)	(5,997,660.75)
	Balance, end of the year	6,287,783.75	11,699,503.00
	Total Fund	**12,828,463.75**	**22,334,716.97**

11	**Reserve fund**		
	Balance, beginning of year	----------	430,000
	Transfer from appropriation	430,000	230,000
	Withdrawal during the year	----------	(1,349,750)
	Balance, end of the year	430,000	(689,750.00)
12	**General Reserve**		
	Balance, beginning of year		797,599.00
	Transfer from appropriation	797,599.00	3,809,867.58
	Withdrawal during the year		(58,000)
	Balance, end of the year	797,599.00	4,549,466.58
13	**Education**		
	Balance, beginning of year		129,000
	Transfer from appropriation	129,000	46,000
	Withdrawal during the year		(258,000)
	Balance, end of the year	129,000	83,000
14	**Land Contribution Fund:**		
	Balance, beginning of year		668,900.00
	Members' contribution for land	668,900.00	2,000,000
	Paid out		(3,851,226.90)
		668,900.00	(1,182,326.90)
15	**Welfare Fund**		
	Balance, beginning of year	----------	61,500
	Members' contribution for land	111,500	191,500
	Paid to members	(50,000)	(133,250)
	Balance, end of the year	61,500	119,250
16	**Membership Strength**	112	100

CHAPTER 11

CO-OPERATIVE REGISTERS

There are four essential registers that every co-operative organization is supposed to keep, namely Assets Register; Shares Register; Members Register; Loan Register.

ASSETS REGISTER

This register helps show details and keep track of all the assets owned by an organization. The features you watch out for in the asset register are the Date the asset was purchased, the Invoice/ payment voucher number, and the name and details of the supplier of the asset. In addition, the disposal of assets and the depreciation rate are used n statements in the accounting policies. Also, the net book value of the assets; The asset number/ serial number; Location of the asset; The name of activity using the asset; Date of disposal if the asset has been sold; the officer responsible for monitoring the asset.

SHARES REGISTER

The share register is vital since it shows evidence of the named shareholder's legal title to the shares in the co-operative, subject to any evidence to the contrary. The cooperative treats the person named in the share register as the registered holder of the relevant shares and the only person entitled to exercise the voting rights that attach to the shares, to receive notices, to receive distributions of dividends in respect of the ratio of the shares holding, and to exercise any other rights and powers that attach to the shares.

The shares register must contain the following information for each class of share: the names, in alphabetical order, and the last known address of each person who currently subscribes to the shares or has been within a certain period determined by the management, a shareholder; the number of shares held by each shareholder within a certain period determined by the management; the date of any issue of shares to each shareholder within a certain period determined by the management; the date of any transfer of shares by or to each shareholder within a certain period determine by the management, including the name of the other party to the transfer

MEMBERS REGISTER
This register shows the number of members that the co-operative Society has since inception and the numbers that have resigned or withdrawn their members or relocated from the co-operative area of operations. It is an essential document in a Co-operative regarding knowing the bonafide members. Therefore, it must be kept at the Co-operative's registered office and updated as appropriate. In addition, it should be available for inspections by the members.

The member's register must contain the following information: The full name of the member; the phone number of the member; the next of kins of the member; The date when they joined the co-operative; The address of the member; The number of shares held by the member; The occupation of the member; The place of domicile; The nationality of the member; passport of the member; bank details of the members.

LOAN REGISTER
It is a source document containing information regarding all loans granted at any time by the management committee or credit or loan committee meeting. Such information includes personal membership number; member identity number,

committee meeting minute number; cheque number, amount authorized and approved; amount applied for; Amount granted, date of approval, period of the loan, and date of refund. This schedule will also be used to post the cash book and member personal account. The total figure on the cheque schedule will also be used for direct casting to the society's check register. Authority to pay out when the credit or loan committee approves a loan is by the chairman and member of the credit or loan committee signing on the application form. Cheque signatories on the cheque schedule endorse further approval of check payment. All the cheques must be individually listed on the cash receipt, cash disbursement journal and cash journal.

CHAPTER 12

SHARING OF ANNUAL DIVIDEND, INTEREST ON SAVING AND BONUS

In a cooperative society, as you save and access, every member should also share from the surplus declared at the end of the financial year. The co-operative society reported surplus, not profit since they are exempted from paying company income tax. Company income tax is based on the company that declared profit.

When a cooperative society makes a surplus, it is shared based on the sharing formula approved by the bye-law. Based on the Bye-Law of Port Harcourt United Fortune Investment & Credit Society Limited Bye-Law and in compliance with the Bye-Laws (as amended), the net surplus of the Society shall be appropriated as follows:

Disposal of Surplus

i) Reserve Fund: 10% shall be carried to the Reserve fund
ii) Education Fund shall have 2% of the surplus
iii) And the balance to be appropriated for the following
iv) Management Committee of not more than 10% of the net surplus.
v) Building up a General Reserve
vi) Payment of a dividend on shares shall be 30% of the declared surplus.
vii) Payment of bonus to members as a refund of a percentage of interest paid on loan during the year shall be 28%.
viii) Payment of Interest on savings shall be 20% of surplus
ix) Donations not exceeding 2% of the net surplus shall

be made to charitable organization(s) annually for social welfare approved by the Director;

x) Building up a General Reserve

Based on the disposal of surplus, we have seen above, we can assume figures and get the way co-operative should share its surplus accordingly.

ILLUSTRATION

Assume the Co-operative Society declared as surplus of $176. The book is able to determine how the declared dividend and others will be distributed among the list below;

1. Dividend -30%: Those that have shares i.e. shareholders. This is what make one become a member
2. Savings-20%: Those that have savings.
3. Bonus-28%: Those that have taken loan and participate in all the sales
4. Honoraria-10%: This is for the management executive committee
5. Reserve -10%: This is for reserve for raining day
6. Education-2%: This is for education, and members training.

DETERMINE TOTAL SHARES AND TOTAL SAVINGS

The first thing to do is to determine the total number of shares owned by every member. You will need to get the names of all the members and associated shares to each of them. Then summed together and also get the fraction of each member's share to the total number of shares (see column A below) and each member's savings to total savings (see column B below). This will enable management to prepare what each member is entitled to at the end of the year. The sharing formula determines the level of risk associated to each member. This is in line with Modern Portfolio Theory (MPT). MPT is an investment theory that permits a member of the society to contribute to both share and savings to

CO-OPERATIVE SOCIETY MANAGEMENT AND ACCOUNTING SYSTEM

maximize the expected return for a given level of risk associated with their investment. According to the MPT, a member must be rewarded for investing more in the co-operative with higher expected returns. The expected return comes from dividends, interest on savings and bonuses for accessing loans. MPT focus on diversification of investment in shares and savings.

$176		30% Dividend (A)	20% Interest (B)	10% Committe(C)	D=A+B+C	Interest Paid	28% Bonus(E)	F=D+E	10% R/fund	2% Edu. F
	Shares	$52.8	Savings $35.2	$17.6			$49.3		$17.6	$3.52
MR A	300	10.5	700.0 16.21	7		34	20	17.9	52	
MR B	150	5.3	150.0 3.47			9			9	
MR C	278	9.7	1,800.0 41.69			51	10	9.0	60	
MR D	264	9.3	246.0 5.70			15			15	
MR E	334	11.7	49.0 1.13	5		18			18	
MR F	300	10.5	600.0 13.90	5		30	20	17.9	48	
MR G	165	5.8	135.0 3.13			9			9	
MR H	180	6.3	180.0 4.17			10	5	4.5	15	
MR I	132	4.6	68.0 1.57			6			6	
MR J	330	11.6	30.0 0.69			12			12	
MR K	120	4.2	60.0 1.39			6			6	
MR L	300	10.5	300.0 6.95			17			17	
	2,853	100	4,318 100	18		218	55	49	267	18	4

From the table above, the sum of $176 in yellow was declared as a surplus to distribute to twelve members from A to L. The amount allocated for dividend, interest, management committee are $52.8, $35.2 and $17.6 respectively. Also, $49.3 was appropriated to Bonus for members that obtained loan from the co-operative in the year under review. The column F revealed the total every member is expected to receive at the end of the financial year.

CHAPTER 13

FINAL REPORT FROM MEMBERS CONTRIBUTION

The input is the member's contribution to the financial report, which is the output. One crucial thing in co-operative management is recording all transactions and producing a timely financial statement. Moreover, the fraction of each member's share contribution (see column A above) and each member's savings contribution (see column B above) will be apparent if the management of the co-operative tabulates it on the individual member contribution table below.

INDIVIDUAL MEMBER CONTRIBUTIONS

Reg No	Names	Commitment	Extrance	January Shares	January Savings	February Shares	February Savings	March Shares	March Savings	Payments Savings withdrawal	Total Contribution	Total Shares	Max share 20% share	Total Savings	no limit share no limit
1	MR A	$400.0	10	100	300	100	300	100	300	200	1,000	300	10.51525	700	16.211209
2	MR B	$100.0	10	50	50	50	50	50	50		300	150	5.257624	150	3.4738305
3	MR C	$700.0	10	100	600	100	600	100	600	22	2,078	278	9.744129	1,800	41.685966
4	MR D	$170.0	10	88	82	88	82	88	82		510	264	9.253417	246	5.697082
5	MR E	$161.0	10	128	33	128	33	128	33	100	383	334	11.70698	49	1.1347846
6	MR F	$300.0	10	100	200	100	200	100	200		900	300	10.51525	600	13.895322
7	MR G	$100.0	10	55	45	55	45	55	45		300	165	5.783386	135	3.1264474
8	MR H	$120.0	10	60	60	60	60	60	60		360	180	6.309148	180	4.1685966
9	MR I	$100.0	10	44	56	44	56	44	56	100	200	132	4.626709	68	1.5748031
10	MR J	$120.0	10	110	10	110	10	110	10		360	330	11.56677	30	0.6947661
11	MR K	$60.0	10	40	20	40	20	40	20		180	120	4.206099	60	1.3895322
12	MR L	$200.0	10	100	100	100	100	100	100		600	300	10.51525	300	6.947661
			120	975	1,556	975	1,556	975	1,556	422	7,171	2,853	100	4,318	100

The table above shows individual members' contributions, their share of total contributions, contribution withdrawal and their contribution balance in the co-operative. Designing such a template with the help of excel will help the management of the co-operative to keep track of the total contribution by each member from inception to date. The table is self-explanatory; individual figures can be transferred to the share, savings contribution, and withdrawal account below.

In addition, determine members' total withdrawal from contribution for personal use and ascertain their current balances in the co-operative. The table below can clarify such transactions.

Shares Contribution

S/n	Date	ref. N	Particulars	Oustanding	Cash	$	
1	Jan		Jan		975.00	975.00	
2	Feb		Feb		975.00	975.00	
3	Mar		Mar		975.00	975.00	
4					2,925.00	2,925.00	
5			withdrawal		72.00	72.00	
				0.00	2,853.00	2,853.00	0.00

Savings Contribution

S/n	Date	ref. N	Particulars	Oustanding	Cash	$	
1	Jan		Jan		1,556.00	1,556.00	
2	Feb		Feb		1,556.00	1,556.00	
3	Mar		Mar		1,556.00	1,556.00	
4					4,668.00	4,668.00	
5			withdrawal		350.00	350.00	
				0.00	4,318.00	4,318.00	

Withdrawal

S/n	Date	ref. N	Particulars	Shares	Savings	$
1	Jan		Mr A		200.00	200.00
2	Jan		Mr C	22.00		22.00
3	Feb		Mr E	50.00	50.00	100.00
4	Mar		Mr I		100.00	100.00
				72.00	350.00	422.00

The table above shows the share contribution, saving contribution and withdrawal ledger to keep track of the records and ensure future reference. From this point, the balancing figure can be posted on the financial statement. The share contribution and saving contribution after deducting the withdrawal from savings make up the total member's contribution which will appear in the statement of financial position under the accumulated fund.

DR FRIDAY OJEABURU

S/n	Date	ref. No	Particulars	Loan Account DR Side(Received)	CR Side(Pay	Amount ($)	Interest paid	Member loan balance
1	Jan		MR A	2,500.0		2,500.0	20.0	
2	Jan		MR C	1,250.0		1,250.0	10.0	
3	Feb		MR F	2,500.0		2,500.0	20.0	
4	Feb		MR A		208.0	-208.0		
5	Feb		MR C		104.0	-104.0		
6	Mar		MR H	1,625.0		1,625.0	13.0	1,625.0
7	Mar		MR A		208.0	-208.0		2,084.0
8	Mar		MR C		104.0	-104.0		1,042.0
9	Mar		MR F		208.0	-208.0		2,292.0
				7,875.0	832.0	7,043.0	63.0	7,043.0

The loan account table above will also help track the loan disbursed, the interest received, and the loan's outstanding balance to individual members. This template will enable the co-operative management to keep track of the day-to-day record of the loan to members. This aspect is very complex if not correctly captured, but with this simple template, the co-operative management can know the present state of the loan account at every point. First, the loan balance of $7.043 will be transferred to the statement of financial position. Then, the disbursement of $ 7,875 and $ 832 will be transferred to the cash flow statement. Also, the $63 is the income from the loan given to members, which will be transferred to the statement of income and expenditure (or statement of profit or loss and other comprehensive income). At the same time, the last column is for monitoring the individual balance, which requires addition or subtraction as the case may be

Port Harcourt United Fortune Investment & Credit Society Ltd
21 Emekuku Street, D/Line, Port Harcourt
Income and Expenditure Account for the year ended

		Year
		$
Revenue		
Interest on Loan		63.00
		120.00
		183.00
Less Expenses:		
Bank Charges		2.00
Administrative Expenses		5.00
Total Expenses		7.00
Suplus (Deficit) for the year		176.00
Appropriation of surplus fund:		
Dividend		52.80
Interest paid to members		35.20
Committee		17.60
Bonus		49.28
Reserve fund		17.60
Education Fund		3.52
		176.00

The table above shows that income and expenditure account (or statement of profit or loss and other comprehensive income). The interest on loan as accumulated from the number of loan disburse to members of the co-operative. Of course, the co-operative is expected to incur expenses which must be paid from the income generated while the balance will be declared as surplus. In co-operative accounting system, there is no profit but surplus because it is not a profit marking organization and it does not pay company income tax to the government.

Statement of Financial Position as at Year Ending		
		$
Non Current Asset		0.00
		0.00
Current Asset		
Cash/Bank		149.12
Loan Account		7,043.00
		7,192.12
Current Liability		
Committee		
Dividend		
Interest paid to members		
		0.00
Net Current Asset		7,192.12
Net Asset		**7,192.12**
Accumulated funds:		
Total Contribution		7,171.00
Reserve fund		17.60
Education Fund		3.52
Net Asset		7,192.12
		0.00

The table above shows the statement of financial position with a net asset of $7,192.12. This also indicates the balances remaining from all the ledgers used in the account preparation. The color yellow above will help to reveal if there is any discrepancy in your account. This will only be possible if you planned your account from individual members' contributions to the financial statement point.

Statement of Cash Flow for the year ended

	Year
	$
Cash Flow from Operating Activities	
Net Profit	176.00
Depreciation	
	176.00
Changes in Working Capital	
Loan Account	-7,043.00
	-6,867.00
Cash Flow from Investing Activities	
Purchase of non current asset	0.00
Cash Flow from Financing Activities	
Total Contribution	7,171.00
Dividend	-52.80
Interest paid to members	-35.20
Committee	-17.60
Bonus	-49.28
	7,016.12
Net cash flow	149.12
Cash C/D	
Cash C/F	**149.12**

In addition, the statement of cash flow shows that cash inflow and cash outflow in the co-operative after which you have a cash c/f of $149.12.

CHAPTER 14

COOPERATIVE INVESTMENT

Nowadays, many cooperatives get involved in purchasing property with the expectation that its value will increase over time. Cooperative investment means the investment of purchasing properties or businesses with the expectation that the value increases over time for the benefit and services of its members. Therefore, cooperatives are the coming together of people with a mutual interest for specific aims and objectives. People like workers working in the same office, craft, trade or work in the same organization etc.

Today in Nigeria, the cooperative is the Investment and Credit Cooperative Society or Credit and Investment Cooperative Society. This type of Cooperative Society started as a Credit Cooperative Society by Abeokuta Catholic Teachers for paying their children's school fees, i.e., pulling part of their mega salary for the said Children's School Fees.

Credit and Investment Cooperative, therefore, means a type of cooperative where everybody saves by pooling resources together. Members can take loans to either buy personal assets, do business, or pay child school fees. Still, there is a bond that the borrowers must benefit from the pool, by that credit and investment cooperative, therefore, have contributed to wealth creation and poverty reduction among the members. The money saved is given out as loan to members, usually twice or thrice of the total member savings, which charge a low-interest rate. For example, some charge 5%, 8%, and 10%, but the cooperative society where I am the pioneer president charged 8%. This pattern of interest has saved someone from the clutches of greedy money lenders who charge a high-interest rate as high as 30% or more to give out loans.

ADVANTAGES OF THIS KIND OF SOCIETY

- Is safe and profitable saving institution.
- Save members from exuberant interest charges
- Saved from delay in obtaining loan from bank
- Saved from default charges from bank when salary is being delay
- Create wealth among members
- Reduce poverty since money are available for members interested
- Increased productivity in their office
- Brought happiness to homes
- Accumulated money for members to start a business since you can take twice of your savings
- It promotes entrepreneurship
- No much collateral is need except a member that must sign for any member obtaining loan.
- Encourage savings habit among members

CHAPTER 15

COOPERATIVE BUDGET

The budget forecasts what the executive management committee hopes to achieve for society in the coming financial year. The budget is a plan for the future. It is an anticipated revenue and expenditure for the society for a particular period, usually one year.

Because the future is full of uncertainties and unforeseen circumstances, a plan must be made to provide safeguards and facilities to ascertain where their business is, what it is doing and how it has to be done. The budgets are the means of control as they reflect performance against plans and offer facilities for the right action. Therefore, budgets are some of the essential tools for planning and coordinating a business organization's activities. Some types of budgets are listed below:

1. **Revenue Budget:** This estimates the numbers of members, and the value of the revenue is expected within a period.
2. **Cost Budget:** This estimates the value of the cost to be run on a particular item for a certain period.
3. **Personnel Budget:** This estimates the total labor requirements necessary to carry out society's activities.
4. **Capital Budget:** The capital budget involves the capital expenditure & may cover several years.
5. **Cash Budget:** The estimated total value of cash coming based on the forecast of the savings and other funds anticipated to be available in the coming year. Since the main object of the society is the mobilization of funds, it is recommended that this section of the budget be prepared monthly. This will enable the

committee to have more accurate forecasts on the funds likely to be available for investment or loans to members.

6. **Master Budget:** This is the central budget that coordinates the organization's activity budgets.

FEATURES OF A GOOD BUDGET
1. It requires full participation of the Co-op society's staff management & members.
2. It normally planned 3 months before the commencement of the financial year.
3. Need approved & consent by the general house.
4. Is simple and easily understandable
5. It covers a time frame of one year.
6. It is flexible & permit adjustments.
7. It allows for changing circumstances.

IMPORTANCE OF BUDGETING
a. **For Planning:** Budget enables organisation to take informed decisions about the future.
b. **Co-ordination: Budget** serves as a vehicle through which the action of the different parts of an organization and activity needs co-ordination so that we can have a full picture of the society/org operation.
c. **Control:** Controlling is the process of making sure that actual performance agrees with what was budgeted.

REASONS FOR BUDGET
a. Budget helps to measure performance with the standards.
b. Budget helps in creation of team work
c. Budget increases individual mind to think to pursuit a set standard.
d. Budget helps in identifying weaknesses in a Co-op society.
e. Budgets which are well formulated & administered facilitate proper communication, fixing responsibilities

& improving good working relationships.

CHAPTER 16

RELEVANT POSTING OF TRANSACTIONS

1. **Financial statement to submit at the annual general meeting (AGM)**
   - ✓ Statement of accounting policies
   - ✓ Auditors report
   - ✓ Management committee report
   - ✓ Statement for financial position
   - ✓ statement of income and expenditure (or statement of profit or loss and other comprehensive income).
   - ✓ Statement of cash flows
   - ✓ Statement of change in equity
   - ✓ Notes to the financial statements
   - ✓ Financial Summary

2. **Account and Records to close every month**
   - ✓ Cash Book
   - ✓ General Ledger (i.e. includes Revenue, Expenses, Loan Disbursed, Loan Repayment etc.)
   - ✓ Analysis Book
   - ✓ Personal Ledger
   - ✓ Members passbook
   - ✓ Loan bond based on request
   - ✓ Cash receipts based on each transaction

3. **Revenue general ledger consist of but not limited to**
   - ✓ Interest on loan
   - ✓ Interest on Salary Advance
   - ✓ Entrance fees

- ✓ Fine & Default fees
- ✓ Admin fees

4. Expenses general leader consist of but not limited to
- ✓ Bank Charges
- ✓ Interest Payable
- ✓ Entertainment Cost
- ✓ Telephone
- ✓ Transport & Travelling
- ✓ Sundry Expenses
- ✓ Office Expenses
- ✓ Honorarium
- ✓ Publicity
- ✓ Discount Allowed

5. Appropriation of surplus
- ✓ Dividend
- ✓ Interest
- ✓ Bonus
- ✓ Education fund
- ✓ General Reserve
- ✓ Revenue Reserve
- ✓ Donation to charitable organization

6. How to post when a member pays $2,000 for entrance fee
Dr. Cash A/c----$2,000
Cr Entrance A/C----$2,000

7. How to post when a member pays $50,000 to be recorded as S20,000 for shares and $30,000 for savings in the member register.
Dr. Bank A/C-----$50,000
Cr Share A/C------$20,000

Cr Savings A/C-----$30,000
Cr Entrance A/C-----$2,000

8. **How to post when a member requested for loan of say $1,000,000 at 8%**
Dr. Loan A/C-----$1,000,000
Cr Bank A/C------$1,000,000
Dr. Loan A/C-------------$80,000
Cr Interest on Loan A/C------$80,000

9. **How to post when a member repays his loan of $1,000,000 in full**
Dr. Bank A/C--------$1,000,000
Cr Loan A/C-------$1,000,000
Dr. Bank A/C--------$80,000
Loan A/C------------$80,000

10. **How to post when a member repays $100,000 as part of his loan of $1,000,000**
Dr. Bank A/C-----------$100,000
Cr Loan A/C---------$20,000
Cr Interest on Loan A/C-----$80,000

11. **When a cooperative pays $100,000 cash for Assets like Furniture, Vehicles etc.**
Dr. Furniture A/C------$100,000
Cr Bank A/C-----------$100,000

12. **Direct Payment of shares and interest.** Example, Grace paid $51,000 by cheque and $ 2,000 in cash to increase her share balances and repay part of the loan as per the following analysis:
Dr. Bank A/C-------$51,000

Dr. Cash A/C--------$2,000
Cr Loan A/C--------$32,000
Loan A/C------------$21,000

In the above case a cash receipt will be written to acknowledge receipt of $53,000
On depositing the $2000 in the bank the following entries will be made:
Dr. Bank A/C------$2,000
Cr Cash A/C------$2,000

13. **Withdrawal/ Termination of Membership Example;**
A member served a written notice of his desire to withdraw from the society. His loan balance stood at $80,000 while his share balance was $92,000. At this point he owes the society the amount of loan + Admin charges 5%of $80,000 ($4,000) and the society owes him $92,000 the difference will be calculated as follows:

Cash journal and personal account as follows:
Dr. Share A/C ----------$92,000
Cr Loan A/C----------$80,000
Cr Admin Fee----------$4,000(5% of $80,000)
Cr Cash A/C------------$8,000(paid to member)

14. **Recording of other incomes**
The society records a cheque of $4,000 being rental income on properly leased out. The society earned interest on fixed deposit account with Co-operative Bank of $ 3,000.
Dr. Bank A/C----------$4,000
Cr Rental Income ----------$4,000
Dr. Bank A/C-------------$3,000
Interest Received A/C-----$3,000

15. **Recording of Expenses Example:** Enter the following transactions into their respective ledger Account in the general ledger book. Co-operative society paid an electricity bill of $16000 with a cheque, sitting allowance of $20,000 to Mr. John in cash and #170,000 was put on a fixed deposit Account at Co-operative bank account.

Dr. Electricity bill A/c---------------$16,000
Cr Bank A/C------------------------$16,000
Dr. Committee sitting allowances---$20,000
Cr Cash A/C------------------------$20,000
Dr. Fixed Deposit A/c ---------------$170,000
Cr Bank A/C---------------------------$170,000

16. **Posting of the Loan Cheque Schedule.** Payment voucher is prepared for the total loan approved. On the basis of the figures Approved the total loan is recorded on the cash disbursement side of the cash journal and individual member account. The entries in the ledger will then appear as follows; Example: The total loan granted as per loan schedule was N610,000 (Grace 200,000 Peter 150,000, Mutahi 250,000 Joan 10,000).

Dr. Loan: Grace------------$200,000
Dr. Loan: Peter--------------$150,000
Dr. Mutahi-------------------$250,000
Dr. Loan: Joan--------------$10,000
Cr Bank A/C-------------------$610,000

✓ Effect the change in the member passbook and personal ledger and also in the analysis book.

17. **How to post when member withdraw N20,000 from his savings free of charge through cheque.**

Dr. Savings A/c of the member -------------$20,000

Cr Bank A/C----------------------------------$20,000
- ✓ Effect the change in the member passbook and personal ledger and also in the analysis book.

18. **How to post when member received dividend of $5,000 into his share without receiving cash or cheque**

First, the trace of the money from appropriation to dividend account need to be established.

Dr. Profit or Loss A/C--------------------------$5,000
Cr Dividend A/C--------------------------------$5,000

Then, also trace how the money enter into member share account.

Dr. Dividend A/C----------------------------------$5,000
Cr Share A/C---------------------------------------$5,000

ABOUT THE AUTHOR

Dr Friday Ojeaburu

Dr Friday Ojeaburu is a seasoned Chartered Accountant who holds a Bachelor of Science (BSc) Degree in Accountancy and Finance from Ambrose Ali University, Master of Science (MSc) Degree in Accounting from University of Port Harcourt and PhD Degree in Financial Accounting from Ignatius Ajuru University of Education, Port Harcourt, Rivers State. He is a full member of both the Institute of Chartered Accountants of Nigeria (ICAN) and Associate member of Nigerian Accounting Association(ANAA) with substantial experience in both the private and public sector spanning over 16 years in financial management, audit & investigation, public sector accounting, environmental accounting, entrepreneurial accounting, career development and online coaching and mentorship et

BOOKS BY THIS AUTHOR

The Pillars That Make Men Great

This book all about how to grow in your business and personal life.

Ultimate Accountant Guide For Job Interview, Students And Beginners: Practical Questions And Answers In Alphabetical Order (Pocket Accounting Words Book 1)

This book is relevant for those training an job interview, employers as well as those who teach accounting in the highest institution

Multiple Earnings From Ebook Creation And Publishing

This book is about how to write Ebook and earn money from it.

Job Interview Made Easy For Public Sector: Financial Regulations, Public Service Rules And General Paper

This book will be useful for those writing job interview in government office

Marketable Resumes

This book shown the best way to write resume.

www.ingramcontent.com/pod-product-compliance
Lightning Source LLC
Chambersburg PA
CBHW070119230526
45472CB00004B/1335